4

5

7

THEY CAN'T BE THINKING OF STEALING THESE ROLES AWAY FROM US, LIKE THEY DID WITH TWINKLE TOWNE, I HOPE?!

WELL... THEY DIDN'T REALLY... STEAL THEM. I MEAN, THEY WERE... YOU KNOW...

'GOOD' ISN'T THE WORD YOU'RE LOOKING FOR, RIGHT, LITTLE BROTHER?

NO, NO, IT'S...

LUCKY! THEY WERE LUCKY! IT WAS JUST CHANCE, A FLUKE, A COINCIDENCE, A ONCE-IN-A-LIFETIME TWIST OF FATE, GOT IT?

AS CLEAR AS DAY.

GOOD! AND NOW, RYAN, GIVEN THAT YOU'RE THE CHOREOGRAPHER, YOU NEED TO CONCENTRATE ON THE MOST IMPORTANT ASPECT OF THE MUSICAL.

DANCE?

NO! ME!

IN ANY CASE, THOSE TWO ARE UP TO **SOMETHING**. WE'D BETTER KEEP OUR EYES ON THEM.

I DIDN'T KNOW WHAT TO SAY, EITHER, WHEN TAYLOR ASKED ME...

BUT YOU **LIKED** SINGING TOGETHER, DIDN'T YOU?

"IT WAS WONDERFUL, TROY! I REALLY FELT LIKE MYSELF UP ON STAGE WITH YOU."

BUT I'M CONFUSED. THEY'RE EXPECTING TOO MUCH OF ME. MAYBE I'M...

...MAYBE I'M NOT GOOD ENOUGH, I MIGHT DISAPPOINT THEM, IT MIGHT ALL HAVE BEEN...

...JUST A **FLUKE**. YEAH. WHEN WE SING TOGETHER, WE'RE SOMETHING SPECIAL, BUT...

I LIKE THIS PLACE. I LIKE THAT WE'VE GOT OUR OWN SECRET GARDEN HERE AT SCHOOL...

13

IT WASN'T AN EASY DECISION...

BUT I'VE FOUND OUR JEAN-LUC AND SIMONE.

THE ROLE OF THE MALE LEAD, THE PAINTER IN SEARCH OF HIS MUSE, GOES TO **TROY BOLTON**!

WAY TO GO, BUD!

THE ROLE OF JEAN-LUC'S MUSE, HIS ONE TRUE **LOVE**...

...SIMONE, THE FEMALE LEAD...

MS. DARBUS, I OFFICIALLY PROTEST! AS PRESIDENT OF THE DRAMA CLUB, I'D LIKE TO PUT AN END TO THIS **INJUSTICE**!

...GOES TO THE EXTRAORDINARY SHARPAY EVANS!

YEEAH! YESSSS! EXTRAORDINARY! I KNEW IT!

THE ROLE OF ARMAND, SIMONE'S BROTHER, GOES TO OUR CHOREOGRAPHER, RYAN EVANS.

I... I'M SORRY! I DON'T KNOW HOW THIS COULD'VE HAPPENED.

IT DOESN'T MATTER... REALLY.

IF YOU AREN'T IN IT, I **WON'T** BE IN IT, EITHER!

BUT THEN YOU'D HAVE WASTED ALL THOSE HOURS WE SPENT REHEARSING.

BUT THERE'S GOT TO BE A WAY...

THERE'S STILL ONE MORE ROLE TO ASSIGN...

THANKS TO A CLOSE FRIENDSHIP I FORMED BACK AT MY UNIVERSITY'S SHAKESPEARE CLUB...

FRANK ROPERS, AN IMPORTANT THEATRICAL **TALENT SCOUT** FROM LOS ANGELES...

...WILL BE COMING TO SEE OUR MUSICAL!

THERE'S NO NEED FOR ME TO EXPLAIN HOW IMPORTANT THIS NEWS IS, OR THE FACT THAT YOUR WORK...

BE IT DIRECTING

OR SINGING

OR DANCING

OR PLAYING MUSIC

OR EVEN JUST WORKING ON THE STAGE DESIGN AND MANAGING TH PRODUCTION...

...WILL BE JUDGED BY A PROFESSIONAL FOR THE FIRST TIME.

IT'LL BE UP TO YOU TO SHOW YOU'RE **WORTHY** OF THIS OPPORTUNITY.

21

Episode Two:

"THE BATTLE OF THE REHEARSALS"

YOU THINK SHE'S RIGHT?

GUYS, WE'VE GOT THE ANSWER! A GAME, GUYS AGAINST GIRLS! BUT THEY WON'T EVEN MAKE A **SINGLE** SHOT!

WE'LL SEE ABOUT **THAT**, WON'T WE, GABRIELLA?

?

DO YOU THINK YOUR PLAN WILL WORK?

OF COURSE! EITHER THEY'LL LEARN TO PLAY ACCORDING TO **MY** RULES OR THEY WON'T PLAY AT ALL!

WELL, THEN, IF TROY WON'T BE PLAYING JEAN-LUC... I COULD DO IT...

THE ONLY ROLE THAT COUNTS IS **SIMONE**! ROPERS SHOULD ONLY SEE HER ON STAGE!

AND YOU'RE SIMONE'S CHOREOGRAPHER, RYAN. TRY NOT TO FORGET IT!

OKAY. WHERE ARE WE GOING, SIMONE?

28

I'VE GOT HER! I'VE GOT HER!

NICE GOING, JASON! GOOD THING I'M HERE...

YOU'RE RIGHT, CHAD...

IT'S A GOOD THING YOU'RE HERE!

YES! TWO POINTS ONCE AGAIN, MR. DANFORTH!

OH, MAN!

THEY WON'T MAKE A **SINGLE SHOT**, HUH?

SHUT YOUR TRAP, CAPTAIN! YOU TOO, JASON!

WHAT DID I SAY?

GUYS! **BAD NEWS!**

"...BACKSTAGE AWAITS!"

Episode Three:

"BACKSTAGE SPIRIT"

EAST HIGH, AUDITORIUM, A LITTLE WHILE LATER.

YOU'RE BENT ON RUINING THIS SHOW, AREN'T YOU?

WHAT DID I DO?

MS. DARBUS, WILL THESE FILTERS BE ENOUGH TO LIGHT UP SHARPAY?

I THINK A SIMPLE WHITE LIGHT WILL BE ENOUGH, MR. BAYLOR!

"WHAT DID I DO?" LET ME EXPLAIN. THIS IS A MUSICAL ABOUT IMPRESSIONIST PAINTERS, SET IN THE YEAR 1874...

SO HOW CAN THERE BE THE EIFFEL TOWER IF THEY STARTED BUILDING IT IN 1887?

YOU'VE GOT A POINT... BUT SINCE I'VE ALREADY FINISHED, WE MIGHT AS WELL USE IT ANYWAY!

COME ON, CAN'T YOU EVEN CRACK A SMILE?

HEY... EVERYTHING OKAY? I'VE BEEN TRYING TO GET IN TOUCH WITH YOU SINCE YESTERDAY...

I WAS BUSY WITH THE SCRIPT AND HAD MY CELL OFF, TROY.

38

CAN'T STAND THIS MUSICAL ANYMORE...

THIS CHOREOGRAPHY IS RIDICULOUS!

BUT THE JAZZ SQUARE IS A CLASSIC STEP, EVERYBODY ADORES IT!

WELL, I DON'T! AND TROY'S HEAD'S IN THE CLOUDS TODAY... CO-DIRECTOR MONTEZ, WOULD YOU PLEASE SAY SOMETHING TO HIM?

YOU MAY HAVE A POINT... TROY, YOU'RE NOT REALLY DOING YOUR BEST TODAY.

SEE? YOU SHOULD AT LEAST **TRY** TO WORK UP TO MY LEVEL!

RIGHT, I SHOULD...

COME ON, ZEKE! QUIT LIGHTING UP EVERYONE BUT ME!

I'LL TAKE CARE OF EVERYTHING, SHARPAY!

NO, BUDDY, I'LL TAKE CARE OF EVERYTHING! CHECK OUT WHAT HAPPENS WHEN THE DOOR OF CAFÉ SOLEIL OPENS...

I CAN'T BELIEVE IT... I DON'T WANT TO BELIEVE IT!

"DID YOU GUYS TALK ABOUT IT THAT AFTERNOON

NO, HE WAS SUPPOSED TO SING WITH SHARPAY AND I WAS SUPPOSED TO WORK ON THE CHOREOGRAPHY WITH RYAN.

AND THE NEXT DAY?

NOTHING... DOING MORE PRACTICE, TESTS, PRACTICE, TESTS...

EVEN IF WE WANTED TO, WE'D HAVE A HARD TIME AVOIDING EACH OTHER THE WAY WE ARE NOW!

AST HIGH, MISTRY CLASS, WEEK LATER.

DON'T TALK THAT WAY. YOU'RE GABRIELLA AND TROY, THE HOTTEST COUPLE AT EAST HIGH!

YEAH, EVERYBODY SEEMS TO THINK SO, BUT...

...BUT WHAT IF WE WEREN'T ANYMORE?

DON'T YOU THINK YOU'RE GOING SLIGHTLY OVERBOARD?

MAYBE... MAYBE NOT. THIS MUSICAL IS TAKING UP SO MUCH OF OUR TIME THAT THERE'S NONE LEFT FOR US.

"TAKE YESTERDAY, FOR EXAMPLE..."

"OR THE DAY BEFORE..."

...T HIGH,
...ER ON.

I SAY IT'S A LOUSY IDEA! IT'S NOT LIKE IT WAS A DATE OR ANYTHING...

OF COURSE, IT'S A DATE. FLOWERS AND CAKES ARE PERFECT, GIRLS LOVE 'EM... AND THEY LOVE BASKETBALL PLAYERS, TOO!

I DIDN'T HAVE TO PLAY AGAINST TAYLOR IN THE FINALS! PLEASE, ZEKE, HELP ME...

I AM HELPING YOU!

CHILL OUT, CHAD. YOU WEREN'T THIS NERVOUS BEFORE THE LEAGUE CHAMPIONSHIP FINALS!

TAYLOR?

TAYLOR, IT'S ME, CHAD. IF YOU'RE NOT HERE, I'M HISTORY - I'VE GOT A GAME LATER.

YOUR GAME CAN WAIT, CHAD. I CAN'T. WE HAVE TO TALK.

45

I NEVER EVER WANT TO SEE HIM AGAIN.

COME ON, DON'T TALK THAT WAY... IT WAS AN ACCIDENT...

NO, IT WASN'T! HE'D PLANNED TO PLAY A TRICK ON SHARPAY... AND THAT INCLUDED MESSING UP MY WORK, AS USUAL!

YEAH, BUT YOU YOURSELF SAID HE WAS TRYING TO SAVE YOU FROM GETTING DOUSED WITH PAINT...

THAT DOESN'T COUNT FOR MUCH, MARTHA. LOOK AT THIS! MY HAIR WILL NEVER BE THE SAME.

WELL, WHAT'S UP WITH YOU TWO?

PFFFT

PFFFT

HA-HA-HA!

I'M SPEECHLESS...

47

YOU THINK IT'S FUNNY? WELL, IT'S NOT. AND NEITHER WERE THOSE PAINTINGS ON THE SCENERY BACKGROUNDS, OR THE BASKETBALL HOOP IN A PARIS CAFÉ...

TAYLOR...

LOOK AT YOURSELF. PRETTY AMUSING, ISN'T IT?

I THOUGHT THE SCENERY PAINTINGS AND THE BASKETBALL HOOP WERE A HOOT, TOO! CHAD KNOWS HOW TO KEEP US LAUGHING WHEN WE'RE HARD AT WORK ON THE MUSICAL...

YOU SHOULD LOOK AT THE FUNNY SIDE OF THINGS, GIRL - NOT JUST THE SERIOUS SIDE.

THAT GOES DOUBLE FOR ME, THANK YOU.

HE-HE-HA-HA!

I REALLY BLEW IT...

NO, YOU DIDN'T, BUDDY. NO BIG LOSS. YOU CAN ALWAYS MAKE UP FOR IT...

THIS'LL MAKE HER EVEN MADDER, I KNOW HER.

TAYLOR'S TOTALLY INTO THIS MUSICAL AND HER JOB IN IT. YOU'VE GOT TO SHOW HER SHE CAN COUNT ON YOU.

NO, YOU CAN HAVE FUN AND BE COMMITTED AT THE SAME TIME! YOU'RE CHAD, YOU CAN DO IT!

YOU MEAN, STOP HAVING A GOOD TIME...

YOU TALK TO GABRIELLA?

NOT YET, BUT... I KNOW HOW TO STRAIGHTEN THINGS OUT WITH HER.

NOW?

KNOW WHAT I SAY? LET'S GO SEE WHAT THEY'RE UP TO... RIGHT NOW!

NOW! GO TO HIM AND TELL HIM **EVERYTHING**! YOU TWO WERE MADE FOR EACH OTHER, YOU'LL WORK IT OUT. I'M SURE.

I DUNNO. I'D LIKE TO BELIEVE IT. I'D LIKE TO KEEP BELIEVING IN TROY AND IN GABRIELLA. I'LL... DO IT!

ALRIGHT! I'LL GO GET CHAD. BUT FIRST I NEED A FAVOUR FROM ZEKE...

TAYLOR, HEY... I'M REALLY SORRY. I DON'T WANT TO COMPLICATE THINGS FOR YOU. I'LL HELP OUT, I'LL WORK BACKSTAGE WITH YOU.

TROY! TROY, WAIT! I'VE GOT TO TELL YOU SOMETHING...

HA-HA-HA!

I REALLY APPRECIATE YOUR APOLOGY, CHAD. AND I APPRECIATE WHAT YOU DID. NOW I KNOW WHERE I WENT WRONG...

MS. DARBUS, I'D LIKE GABRIELLA TO REPLACE SHARPAY IN THE MUSICAL. I'D LIKE US TO SING TOGETHER.

WHAT ARE YOU DOING, TROY? YOU HAVE NO IDEA... WHAT YOU'RE SAYING...

GABRIELLA! HOLD ON!

WAIT!

LET ME GO, TROY.

WHAT HAPPENED? WHAT'S GOING ON WITH YOU?

I HEARD YOU ASK MS. DARBUS TO LET ME SING WITH YOU INSTEAD OF SHARPAY...

YEAH... I... THOUGHT YOU WERE INTO IT, TOO...

BUT THAT MEANS I'D GIVE UP BEING CO-DIRECTOR.

IT'S IMPORTANT TO ME...I THOUGHT YOU KNEW...

I KNOW, BUT EVER SINCE THIS MUSICAL, THINGS BETWEEN US HAVE ONLY GOTTEN WORSE...

I JUST WANT TO FIX EVERYTHING. DON'T YOU?

LATER ON, IN THE AUDITORIUM.

ALL RIGHT! I BURNED YOU AGAIN!

MAYBE I LET YOU. EVER THINK OF THAT?

YEAH, RIGHT! IT'S THE LEAST YOU COULD DO, IF YOU WANNA BE MY GUY!

WHAT'S THAT HOOP DOING THERE?

HOOP, SHARPAY? NO HOOP HERE! SEE?

ANYWAY, THE SETS ARE ALL FINISHED!

HA, HA!

SHE JUST DOESN'T KNOW HOW TO HAVE A GOOD TIME!

WHAT KIND OF DANCE NUMBERS ARE THESE?

IMPROVED, BUT YOU CAN DO BETTER.

HEY!

STUMP

I WORKED ALL DAY ON THIS STUFF! THIS IS SOME **COMPLICATED** CHOREOGRAPHY!

I KNOW YOU, RYAN. YOU'RE HOLDING BACK.

YOU'D BETTER REFLECT ON THE KIND OF COMMITMENT YOU'RE PUTTING INTO MY MUSICAL!

DON'T TAKE IT SO HARD, YOU KNOW HOW YOUR SISTER IS... SHE KEEPS CALLING IT **HER** MUSICAL!

THEY COULD BE BETTER, KELSI, SHE'S RIGHT ABOUT THAT.

REALLY... YOUR DANCE NUMBERS ARE GREAT... PERFECT FOR MY SONGS!

"STILL THE PITS, HUH?"

IT'S A REAL MESS BETWEEN US. I CAN'T EVEN SING ANYMORE...

THAT'S NOT SURPRISING!

THE NEXT MORNING.

YOU HAVEN'T BEEN YOURSELVES SINCE YOUR FIGHT. TO ME, THAT MEANS YOU'RE REALLY IMPORTANT TO EACH OTHER!

I DON'T KNOW. IT SEEMS THAT IF WE DON'T SING TOGETHER, WE CAN'T STAY TOGETHER!

THE WORST PART OF IT IS... I MISS HER.

I REALLY MISS HIM...

...BUT I DON'T WANT TO GIVE UP CO-DIRECTING. THAT WOULDN'T BE FAIR...

MAYBE YOU TWO ARE JUST A LITTLE CONFUSED...

A LITTLE? ALL I'VE BEEN THINKING ABOUT ARE THE SONGS, THE COSTUMES AND EVERYTHING ELSE, WHILE HE'S WRAPPED UP IN HIS ROLE AS JEAN-LUC.

I KNOW, BUT YOU SHOULDN'T LET THAT COME BETWEEN YOU, GABRIELLA...

OKAY, ORIGINAL CHOREOGRAPHY... UNIQUE... I CAN DO IT!

NOTHING! MY INSPIRATION IS COMPLETELY GONE...

MAYBE HE NEEDS A VACATION.

OOPS! SORRY, I JUST NEEDED A QUIET PLACE...

DON'T SWEAT IT, KELSI COMES HERE EARLY TO PRACTISE, TOO. AND I USUALLY COME TO LISTEN.

BUT TODAY WE'VE GOT SOMETHING ELSE ON THE MENU... WHY NOT TAG ALONG?

?

"ROY AND GABRIELLA STILL AREN'T SPEAKING TO EACH OTHER..."

EAST HIGH, THE DAY BEFORE OPENING NIGHT.

I'M SURE THEY'LL GET IT TOGETHER FOR TOMORROW NIGHT... THEY HAVE TO!

YEAH, I HOPE THEY WILL...

ANYWAY, THANKS FOR THE SCOOP... NOW THAT I'VE FINISHED UP WITH THE SCENERY, I MISS REHEARSAL!

YEAH, ME TOO... INCREDIBLE!

RING RING

RING

HEY... A TEXT MESSAGE FROM DARBUS!

OH, NO...

THE STAGE... THE STAGE HAS BEEN...

THERE'S NOTHING WE CAN DO ABOUT IT. I'LL HAVE TO CALL THE AGENT, FRANK ROPERS, AND TELL HIM NOT TO COME TOMORROW NIGHT. HOW AWFUL...

IT'S NO BIGGIE, MS. DARBUS...

THIS MUSICAL'S BEEN A DREAM AND A NIGHTMARE AT THE SAME TIME. AT LEAST IT'S FINALLY OVER...

NO! WE CAN DO THIS... WE CAN... BUT WE HAVE TO WORK TOGETHER!

...MAYBE IT'S BETTER THIS WAY!

IT'S NO USE, I'M TELLIN' YOU!

NO, IT'S NOT "NO USE", ZEKE!

GABRIELLA, LISTEN... MAYBE WE SHOULD JUST FORGET ABOUT IT.

"FORGET ABOUT IT"? DO YOU JUST WANT TO THROW AWAY ALL THE TIME AND ENERGY YOU'VE PUT INTO THIS MUSICAL?

NOBODY WANTS TO DO THAT, BUT WE DON'T HAVE ANY OTHER CHOICE!

I THINK WE DO!

MS. DARBUS? TELL MR. ROPERS HE'D BETTER COME TOMORROW NIGHT... THE MUSICAL IS ON!

MISS MONTEZ, I APPRECIATE YOUR SPIRIT, BUT I BEG YOU TO TAKE A LOOK AROUND. WE CAN'T POSSIBLY REBUILD EVERYTHING ON SUCH SHORT NOTICE.

WE CAN DO IT IF WE ALL WORK TOGETHER... AND IF WE'RE GIVEN PERMISSION TO DO IT TONIGHT!

ARE YOU PROPOSING A "LOCK-IN NIGHT"... TO PUT THE STAGE BACK IN ORDER?

AND THE COSTUMES AND THE LIGHTS AND EVERYTHING ELSE! MS. DARBUS SAID SO HERSELF... THEATRE REQUIRES ENTHUSIASM AND COMMITMENT...

Episode Five:

"WE'RE ALL IN THIS TOGETHER"

...AND THERE'S NOTHING THAT CAN STOP US! THIS MUSICAL...

MY MUSICAL!

"TWINKLE SEINE"! IT'S MEANT A LOT TO US... YES! I'M WITH GABRIELLA. WE CAN DO IT!

THIS SEEMS TOTALLY IMPOSSIBLE, THERE'S NO WAY TO DO IT... SO I SAY WE GO FOR IT!

OKAY... LET'S DO IT!

"SO THE SHOW GOES ON, TOMORROW NIGHT?"

COME ON, KIDS! WE'VE GOT A LONG NIGHT OF HARD WORK AHEAD OF US... FOR THE SAKE OF ART!

ISN'T THIS GREAT? EVERYBODY WORKING THE WHOLE NIGHT TO SAVE MY CAREER!

I DON'T KNOW HOW TO BREAK THIS TO YOU, SIS, BUT YOU'RE GONNA HAVE TO LEND A HAND AS WELL!

ARE YOU KIDDING? LOOK AT THIS GORGEOUS OUTFIT... AND MY FRESHLY POLISHED NAILS!

PIANO - SETS

COSTUMES

SHARPAY	RYAN
KELSI	MARTHA
TAYLOR	CHAD
ZEKE	JASON
TROY	

RYAN, YOU'VE ALWAYS DONE THE COSTUMES FOR YOUR NUMBERS, SO YOU TAKE CARE OF THE ONES THAT GOT DAMAGED, ALONG WITH MARTHA AND SHARPAY...

ME? TAKE CARE OF THE COSTUMES? NO WAY! I'M A STAR!

SURE, SHARPAY. BUT WHAT'S AN ARTIST WITHOUT THE SHOW?

N-NOTHING?

YOU GOT IT!

KELSI, ZEKE, JASON, YOU GET THE PIANO FROM THE MUSIC ROOM, AND THEN YOU CAN HELP...

...TAYLOR AND CHAD ON THE SETS, ALONG WITH...

"IT'S AS IF FIXING UP THE STAGE..."

"...THE COSTUMES..."

"...THE LIGHTS AND EVERYTHING ELSE..."

"...WAS THE REAL SHOW!"

AHH!

"AND WE'RE LIVING IT... IT'S JUST WHAT WE WANTED, WHAT I WANTED. ONLY NOW... THE ONLY THING I CAN THINK OF..."

ZEKE!

"...IS YOU, TROY. YOU'RE HERE, WITH ME."

SEND OR CANCEL MESSAGE?

MUCH, MUCH LATER...

I CAN'T BELIEVE IT...

...WE DID IT!

I CAN'T FEEL MY HANDS ANYMORE!

THE NEXT TIME ANYONE PROPOSES A MUSICAL, I'M HEADING STRAIGHT FOR THE BASKETBALL COURT!

HEY, I'VE GOT AN IDEA...

SINCE WE'VE FINISHED, WHAT DO YOU GUYS SAY ABOUT...

...HITTING THE CAFETERIA?

THE CAFETERIA?

ARE YOU THINKING WHAT I'M THINKING, KELSI?

IF IT'S CREAMY AND STRAWBERRY FLAVOURED, THEN I THINK WE'RE ON THE SAME TRACK, JASON...

"...FREE ICE CREAM!"

OKAY, JUST ICE CREAM, KIDS! OTHERWISE THE COOK'S LIABLE TO HIT THE ROOF...

HEY, SAVE SOME FOR ME!

GUYS, I CAN'T BELIEVE I'M SAYING THIS... BUT I LOVE SCHOOL!

COOL!

LET'S HEAD FOR THE KITCHEN!

WELL... ON SECOND THOUGHT... ZEKE MADE THAT ICE CREAM FOR TOMORROW! MAYBE WE'RE NOT SUPPOSED TO TOUCH IT...?

INCREDIBLE...

SINCE WE SAVED THE MUSICAL, WE MIGHT AS WELL EAT IT TONIGHT... RIGHT?

YOU MEAN TO SAY WE SHOUL BREAK THE RULE WITH SUCH IMMA BEHAVIOR?

I THINK ZEKE WOULD APPROVE!

I AGWEE COMPWETEWY!

78

STOP DRAGGING ME! I TOLD YOU -- I'M NOT EATING YOUR ICE CREAM UNTIL YOU LEARN TO GIVE ME SOME DECENT LIGHT!

JUST GIVE ME A CHANCE. IF YOU DON'T LIKE IT, I WON'T BOTHER YOU ANY MORE...

...I PROMISE!

NOT FUNNY, ZEKE! TURN IT BACK ON!

AS YOU WISH, SHARPAY!

NO... I CAN'T... BELIEVE IT...

THIS...THIS DOESN'T MEAN THAT YOU STILL DON'T HAVE TO LIGHT ME LIKE A REAL STAR TOMORROW NIGHT!

R-RIGHT! IT'S JUST FOR... GOOD LUCK... YOU DON'T HAVE TO EAT IT IF YOU DON'T WANT...

ARE YOU KIDDING? I'M SO STRESSED ABOUT OPENING NIGHT I COULD EAT THE WHOLE THING!

H-HI...

?

THIS IS THE DUMBEST IDEA YOU'VE EVER HAD, TROY!

MAYBE... BUT IT MIGHT WORK! DON'T HANG UP, OK?

OK

LISTEN... I'M SORRY... I'M SORRY I ASKED YOU TO SING WITH ME, FOR HAVING THOUGHT THE MUSICAL WAS MORE IMPORTANT THAN EVERYTHING ELSE...

I THOUGHT THE SAME THING, TROY... AT LEAST UP UNTIL NOW.

SO WHAT'S CHANGED?

I'VE LEARNED I CAN BE A GOOD DIRECTOR... AND THAT I LIKE THE NEW GABRIELLA...

BUT IF I CAN'T TALK TO YOU, IF I CAN'T SEE YOU, IF I CAN'T BE THAT NEW GABRIELLA WITH YOU, THEN...

I WON'T SING IN "TWINKLE SEINE" IF YOU DON'T SING WITH ME.

YOU KNOW IT'S IMPOSSIBLE. I CAN'T GO ON STAGE.

I DIDN'T ASK YOU TO GO ON STAGE...

...I ASKED YOU TO SING WITH ME.

YOU MEAN...?

YOU KNOW SIMONE'S SONGS, DON'T YOU?

THE BIG MOMENT HAS ARRIVED...

I REALLY THINK THIS IS GOING TO BE A FLOP!

...AND SO HAS THE LAST-MINUTE PANIC!

AN OUTRAGEOUS, UNBELIEVABLE FLOP!

NO, IT'S NOT, TAYLOR, HAVE FAITH!

EVERYTHING'LL GO FINE... AT LEAST I HOPE SO...

RELAX! JUST STAY PROFESSIONAL, EVERYONE!

WHAT DO YOU MEAN? WHAT IF THE SETS BREAK DOWN? WHAT IF NO ONE LIKES THE SHOW?

OR... WHAT IF I FORGET SOMETHING?

WHAT IF I MISS A VERSE?

WHAT IF I BLOW THE LIGHTING?

EXCUSE ME! WHO INVITED EVERYONE TO THE NEGATIVITY PARTY?!?

WHAT IF I MISS A STEP?

YOU CALL THIS 'BEING PROFESSIONAL', RYAN?

HEY GUYS... THE THEATRE AGENT... HE'S HERE!

FRANK ROPERS, SITTING IN THE FRONT ROW!

F-FRONT R-ROW? WHAT'LL WE DO?

THERE'S ONLY ONE THING TO DO, MISS ASSISTANT DIRECTOR...

...PANIC!

MS EVANS!

A TRUE ARTIST MUST NEVER LET HERSELF BE OVERCOME BY STAGE FRIGHT...

BUT MY WHOLE CAREER'S AT STAKE HERE!

I CAN'T REMEMBER A THING... TOTAL VOID, COMPLETE BLACKOUT!

ME TOO!

MAYBE WE'RE NOT READY YET...

DEEP BREATHS, DEEP BREATHS. IT'S NORMAL NOT TO REMEMBER ANYTHING JUST BEFORE THE SHOW. BUT YOU'VE WORKED HARD, I KNOW YOU'RE UP TO IT...

WHATEVER HAPPENS TONIGHT, YOU'VE HONOURED THIS TEMPLE OF ART. I'M PROUD OF YOU!

AND IF STAGE FRIGHT'S THE PROBLEM, CONCENTRATE AND IMAGINE THAT EVERYTHING TURNS OUT FINE... BELIEVE ME, IT WORKS!

CAN YOU GUYS DO IT?

NO WAY!

SHE'S RIGHT, YOU KNOW. THIS IS OUR BIG CHANCE! IT'S OUR MUSICAL, AND WE'RE GOING TO GIVE IT OUR BEST SHOT... WITHOUT BEING AFRAID.

ARE YOU WITH ME?

"I DID JUST AS MS DARBUS SAID..."

WELCOME TO THE SHOW, FRANK.

"EVERYBODY'S OUT THERE. FRANK ROPERS, THE PRINCIPAL, MY MOTHER..."

"MY HEART WAS BEATING A MILE A MINUTE!"

"THOUGH I DIDN'T LET IT SHOW..."

WILDCATS!

OK, IT'S SHOWTIME. WHAT TEAM?

"I IMAGINED THAT EVERYTHING WOULD GO FINE..."

"...AND IT ACTUALLY WORKED!"

"I DON'T KNOW WHETHER SHARPAY USED THE SAME TACTIC..."

"ZEKE'S LIGHTING WAS GREAT..."

"...SHARPAY HAD NOTHING TO COMPLAIN ABOUT."

"AND THE SCENERY! TAYLOR WAS ON HER GAME!"

CHAD, RAISE NUMBER FIVE! JASON, LOWER NUMBER SIX!

MARTHA, REMEMBER THE UMBRELLA...

"EVERYBODY WAS CONCENTRATING TO THE MAX..."

"...BUT YOU COULD TELL WE WERE ALL HAVING A BALL!"

"THE AUDIENCE WAS FOCUSED ON WHAT WAS HAPPENING ON STAGE."

"THE STORY OF JEAN-LUC, THE IMPRESSIONIST PAINTER, AND HIS BELOVED SIMONE..."

"...WENT DOWN A STORM."

"THE AUDIENCE EVEN GREW ANGRY AS ARMAND FORBADE JEAN-LUC FROM SEEING SIMONE..."

"...AND WAS HAPPY WHEN EVERYTHING WORKED OUT..."

...IT WAS INCREDIBLE!

WHAT ABOUT YOU? DID YOU HAVE A GOOD TIME?

"OH, YEAH!"

ZEKE, SCENE EIGHT. READY WITH THE LIGHTS?

SHARPAY, TROY... SCENE EIGHT, CHANGE COSTUMES... TAYLOR... THE SEINE SCENERY. LET'S MOVE, PEOPLE!

"YOU WERE RIGHT. I WASN'T SURE IT WAS GOING TO WORK, BUT I WAS THERE, BACKSTAGE, WHILE YOU WERE SINGING..."

"...AND I SANG, TOO!"

"I KNOW. AND IT SOUNDS IMPOSSIBLE, BUT I... FELT YOU. AND I KNEW THAT IN REALITY..."

"...YOU WERE ON STAGE WITH ME."

"JUST THE TWO OF US.
NOTHING ELSE..."

"...MATTERED."

95

"THE BEST MUSICAL EVER! I'LL NEVER FORGET IT!"

CLAP CLAP CLAP

THEY'RE APPLAUDING! THEY'RE APPLAUDING!

"NEITHER WILL I, GABRIELLA..."

CLAP CLAP CLAP

"AND NEITHER WILL SHARPAY. SHE GOT MORE BOUQUETS THAN ANYONE ELSE, AND MR ROPERS COMPLIMENTED HER IN PERSON!"

"SPEAKING OF MR ROPERS, WE'D BETTER GO BACK. HE WANTS TO MEET ALL OF US, ESPECIALLY THE ASSISTANT DIRECTOR."

EH

"HE ALSO WANTS TO MEET THE MALE LEAD! DON'T FORGET HOW GREAT YOU WERE..."

BUT THERE'S STILL SOMETHING I HAVE TO DO...